Mindset

Transform Your Thoughts, Transform Your Life: Unlock the Power of a Growth Mindset and Achieve Greater Success, Happiness, and Fulfillment with Mindset

Lance P. Richards

Mindset: Transform Your Thoughts, Transform Your Life: Unlock the Power of a Growth Mindset and Achieve Greater Success, Happiness, and Fulfillment with Mindset

Table of Contents

01: Introduction to Mindset: Understanding the Power of Thoughts..1

02: The Fixed Mindset vs. The Growth Mindset: A Comparison...4

03: Understanding the Impact of Your Mindset on Your Life 8

04: How Your Mindset Shapes Your Perception of Success and Failure..11

05: The Benefits of Adopting a Growth Mindset................14

06: Understanding Your Current Mindset: A Self-Assessment...17

07: Overcoming a Fixed Mindset: Strategies for Change....19

08: The Role of Challenging Yourself in Developing a Growth Mindset..22

09: Embracing Failure as a Path to Growth and Success...24

10: Understanding and Overcoming Negative Thoughts and Beliefs...26

11: Building a Positive Mindset: Strategies for Transformation...29

12: The Power of Gratitude in Shaping Your Mindset.......32

13: Mindfulness: A Key Practice for Mindset Transformation...35

14: The Role of Mindset in Building Strong Relationships.38

15: Mindset and Career Success: How to Reach Your Full

Potential...41

16: Mindset and Financial Abundance: Achieving Your Financial Goals...44

17: The Mindset of a Champion: How to Win in Life and Business...47

18: Mindset and Creativity: Unleashing Your Inner Genius
....50

19: The Mindset of Leadership: Achieving Greatness Through Positive Thinking.......................................53

20: Mindset and Health: The Connection Between Thoughts and Physical Well-Being.....................................56

21: The Mindset of the Entrepreneur: Turning Your Dreams into Reality...59

22: The Mindset of a Learner: A Lifetime of Growth and Development..62

23: Mindset and Resilience: Overcoming Adversity and Hardship..64

24: Mindset and Happiness: Achieving Lasting Joy and Fulfillment...67

25: The Mindset of a Problem Solver: Finding Solutions and Overcoming Obstacles......................................70

26: The Mindset of a Goal-Setter: Achieving Your Dreams and Aspirations..73

27: Mindset and Personal Growth: A Journey to Self-Discovery..76

28: Mindset and Spirituality: Achieving Inner Peace and

Harmony..79

29: The Mindset of a Giver: Living a Life of Service and
Generosity...82

30: Mindset and the Environment: How Your Thoughts Af-
fect the World Around You....................................84

31: The Mindset of Success: Achieving Your Goals and
Dreams..87

32: Mindset and Positive Thinking: The Path to a Better Life
....90

33: Mindset and the Law of Attraction: Attracting What You
Want in Life..92

34: Mindset and Forgiveness: The Key to Inner Peace and
Happiness..95

35: The Mindset of a Champion: Unleashing Your Potential
....98

36: Conclusion: Living a Life of Mindset Mastery............101

Thank You..104

Disclaimer..105

01: Introduction to Mindset: Understanding the Power of Thoughts

The concept of mindset has been widely researched and discussed in the field of psychology and personal development, and it has been proven to play a crucial role in shaping our lives and our experiences. A mindset refers to the set of beliefs, attitudes, and thought patterns that we hold about ourselves, others, and the world around us. These beliefs, attitudes, and thought patterns determine the way we approach life, our relationships, our careers, and even the way we perceive and respond to challenges.

It is important to understand that our mindsets are not set in stone and can be transformed and developed over time. This is where the concept of the growth mindset comes into play. A growth mindset is a belief that our abilities and intelligence can be developed through dedication and hard work. On the other hand, a fixed mindset is the belief that our abilities and intelligence are predetermined and cannot be changed. People with a fixed mindset are more likely to give up easily in the face of challenges, while those with a growth mindset are more likely to persist in the face of adversity and see challenges as opportunities for growth and learning.

Research has shown that a growth mindset is associated with greater success, happiness, and fulfillment, as well as greater resilience in the face of adversity. People with a growth mindset are also more likely to take risks, pursue their passions and dreams, and reach their full potential in life.

The power of our thoughts should not be underestimated. Our thoughts influence the way we feel and the actions we take, and in turn, our actions and experiences shape our thoughts and beliefs. This is why it is so important to be mindful of the thoughts we are thinking and to make a conscious effort to develop a positive and growth-oriented mindset.

In this book, we will delve into the science of mindset, explore the different types of mindsets, and provide practical tools and techniques for developing a growth mindset. We will also explore the connection between mindset and success, happiness, and fulfillment, and provide practical tips for using mindset to transform your life.

01: INTRODUCTION TO MINDSET: UNDERSTANDING THE POWER OF THOUGHTS

In conclusion, mindset plays a crucial role in shaping our lives and experiences, and by understanding the power of our thoughts and developing a growth mindset, we can unlock our full potential and achieve greater success, happiness, and fulfillment in all areas of our lives.

02: The Fixed Mindset vs. The Growth Mindset: A Comparison

The concept of mindset was popularized by psychologist Carol Dweck, who identified two distinct types of mindsets: the fixed mindset and the growth mindset. These two mindsets have different implications for our lives, our success, and our happiness. Understanding the differences between these two mindsets can help us identify which mindset we hold and make the necessary changes to develop a growth mindset.

The Fixed Mindset:

A fixed mindset is characterized by the belief that our abilities, intelligence, and characteristics are predetermined and cannot be changed. People with a fixed mindset are often more concerned with proving their abilities and avoiding failure than with learning and growing. They see challenges as threats to their self-esteem and view failure as a reflection of their lack of ability. This can lead to a fear of taking risks and a reluctance to pursue new opportunities for fear of failure.

The Growth Mindset:

02: THE FIXED MINDSET VS. THE GROWTH MINDSET: A COMPARISON

On the other hand, a growth mindset is characterized by the belief that our abilities and intelligence can be developed through dedication and hard work. People with a growth mindset see challenges as opportunities for growth and learning, and view failure as a natural part of the learning process. They are more likely to take risks, embrace new challenges, and pursue their passions and goals, even in the face of failure. They also tend to have a more positive outlook on life and a greater sense of resilience in the face of adversity.

The Benefits of a Growth Mindset:

Research has shown that a growth mindset is associated with a range of benefits, including greater success, happiness, and fulfillment. People with a growth mindset are more likely to pursue their passions and goals, take risks, and embrace new challenges. They are also more likely to view failure as a learning opportunity and persist in the face of adversity. In addition, they tend to have more positive relationships and a greater sense of personal satisfaction.

The Drawbacks of a Fixed Mindset:

02: THE FIXED MINDSET VS. THE GROWTH MINDSET: A COMPARISON

On the other hand, a fixed mindset can be limiting and can hold us back from reaching our full potential. People with a fixed mindset are more likely to give up easily in the face of challenges and avoid taking risks for fear of failure. They also tend to have lower self-esteem and a negative outlook on life, which can lead to feelings of dissatisfaction and un-happiness.

How to Identify Your Mindset:

To identify your own mindset, it is helpful to reflect on your thoughts and beliefs about yourself, your abilities, and the world around you. Do you believe that your abilities are fixed and cannot be changed, or do you believe that you can develop and improve with effort and hard work? Do you see challenges as threats or as opportunities for growth and learning? Answering these questions can give you insight into your own mindset and help you determine if you have a fixed or growth mindset.

In conclusion, understanding the differences between the fixed mindset and the growth mindset can help us identify our own mindset and make the necessary changes to de-velop a growth mindset. A growth mindset is associated with a range of benefits, including greater success, happiness, and fulfillment, and can help us reach our full potential and achieve our goals and aspirations.

03: Understanding the Impact of Your Mindset on Your Life

Your mindset has a profound impact on your life, shaping your thoughts, beliefs, and actions in ways that can either limit or expand your potential. Your mindset affects not only how you approach challenges and opportunities, but also how you view yourself and the world around you. Understanding the impact of your mindset on your life is an essential step in creating the life you want and achieving your goals and aspirations.

The Power of Thoughts:

Our thoughts shape our beliefs, and our beliefs shape our actions. Our mindset is a reflection of the thoughts and beliefs we hold about ourselves and the world. If we have a fixed mindset, our thoughts and beliefs will be limiting and will hold us back from reaching our full potential. If we have a growth mindset, our thoughts and beliefs will be empowering and will support our growth and development.

The Link between Mindset and Emotions:

Our mindset also has a significant impact on our emotions.

03: UNDERSTANDING THE IMPACT OF YOUR MIND-SET ON YOUR LIFE

People with a fixed mindset tend to have lower self-esteem, negative outlook on life, and are more likely to experience feelings of dissatisfaction and unhappiness. On the other hand, people with a growth mindset tend to have a positive outlook on life and are more likely to experience feelings of happiness and satisfaction.

The Link between Mindset and Behaviors:

Our mindset also affects our behaviors and actions. People with a fixed mindset are more likely to avoid challenges and new opportunities for fear of failure. They are also more likely to give up easily in the face of adversity. On the other hand, people with a growth mindset are more likely to take risks, embrace challenges, and persist in the face of failure.

The Link between Mindset and Success:

Finally, our mindset has a direct impact on our success. People with a growth mindset are more likely to pursue their passions and goals, take risks, and embrace new challenges. They are also more likely to view failure as a learning opportunity and persist in the face of adversity. In addition, they tend to have more positive relationships and a greater sense of personal satisfaction.

In conclusion, our mindset has a powerful impact on our lives, shaping our thoughts, beliefs, emotions, behaviors, and success. Understanding the impact of your mindset on your life is an essential step in creating the life you want and achieving your goals and aspirations. By developing a growth mindset, you can tap into the power of positive thoughts and beliefs and create a life that is filled with greater success, happiness, and fulfillment.

04: How Your Mindset Shapes Your Perception of Success and Failure

Success and failure are two sides of the same coin, and how you perceive them is heavily influenced by your mindset. If you have a fixed mindset, your perception of success and failure will be limited and will hold you back from reaching your full potential. On the other hand, if you have a growth mindset, your perception of success and failure will be empowering and will support your growth and development.

Perception of Success:

People with a fixed mindset often see success as a measure of their innate abilities and qualities. They believe that success is a result of talent and intelligence, and that it is a finite resource that cannot be improved upon. This can lead to feelings of inadequacy and low self-esteem when they encounter setbacks or failures.

People with a growth mindset, on the other hand, see success as a result of hard work, effort, and persistence. They believe that they can improve their abilities and qualities through effort and learning, and that success is an ongoing process of growth and development. This mindset allows them to approach setbacks and failures as learning opportunities, and to view success as a journey rather than a destination.

Perception of Failure:

People with a fixed mindset often view failure as a measure of their worth and abilities. They believe that failure is a reflection of their innate limitations and that it is something to be ashamed of. This can lead to feelings of discouragement and a reluctance to take risks or embrace challenges.

People with a growth mindset, on the other hand, view failure as a necessary part of the learning process. They believe that failure is an opportunity for growth and development, and that it is an essential step on the road to success. This mindset allows them to approach failures with a positive attitude, and to see them as opportunities for learning and growth.

The Impact of Mindset on Performance:

Your mindset can also impact your performance in both

04: HOW YOUR MINDSET SHAPES YOUR PERCEPTION OF SUCCESS AND FAILURE

personal and professional settings. People with a fixed mindset are more likely to avoid challenges and opportunities for fear of failure. They are also more likely to give up easily in the face of adversity. On the other hand, people with a growth mindset are more likely to take risks, embrace challenges, and persist in the face of failure. This can have a significant impact on their performance, as well as their overall success and satisfaction in life.

In conclusion, your mindset shapes your perception of success and failure in profound ways. If you have a growth mindset, your perception of success and failure will be empowering and will support your growth and development. By embracing a growth mindset, you can tap into the power of positive thoughts and beliefs and create a life that is filled with greater success, happiness, and fulfillment.

05: The Benefits of Adopting a Growth Mindset

Adopting a growth mindset can bring numerous benefits to your life, both personal and professional. This mindset shift can help you unlock your full potential and achieve greater success, happiness, and fulfillment. Some of the key benefits of a growth mindset include:

– Increased motivation and resilience: People with a growth mindset are more motivated to tackle challenges and embrace opportunities, even in the face of setbacks and failures. They are also more resilient, able to bounce back from setbacks and keep going in the pursuit of their goals.

– Better performance: People with a growth mindset are more likely to persist in the face of challenges, take risks, and embrace opportunities. This can lead to improved performance in personal and professional settings, as well as greater success and satisfaction in life.

– Improved relationships: People with a growth mindset are more open to feedback and more likely to seek out constructive criticism. They are also more likely to be supportive and encouraging of others, which can lead to improved relationships and a more positive social network.

– Greater creativity and innovation: People with a growth mindset are more likely to see challenges as opportunities for growth and development. This can lead to greater creativity and innovation, as they are more likely to embrace new ideas and approaches.

– Increased personal growth and development: People with a growth mindset are more likely to view setbacks and failures as learning opportunities. This can lead to greater personal growth and development, as they are more likely to seek out new experiences and embrace new challenges.

– Better mental and emotional well-being: People with a growth mindset are more likely to have a positive outlook on life and to approach challenges with a positive attitude. This can lead to better mental and emotional well-being, as well as greater happiness and fulfillment in life.

In conclusion, adopting a growth mindset can bring numerous benefits to your life. By embracing this mindset, you can tap into the power of positive thoughts and beliefs and create a life that is filled with greater success, happiness, and fulfillment. By shifting your focus from limitations to possibilities, you can unlock your full potential and achieve greater success in all areas of your life.

06: Understanding Your Current Mindset: A Self-Assessment

Before you can start to shift your mindset, it is important to understand your current mindset. By conducting a self-assessment, you can gain insight into your thoughts and beliefs, and determine if you have a fixed or growth mindset.

Here are some questions to help you conduct a self-assessment:

– How do you approach challenges? Do you see them as opportunities for growth and development, or do you avoid them and become discouraged when faced with setbacks?

– How do you handle criticism and feedback? Do you embrace it as a chance for growth, or do you avoid it and become defensive?

– How do you approach failure? Do you see it as a learning opportunity, or do you become discouraged and give up?

– How do you perceive your abilities and skills? Do you believe that they are set and cannot be changed, or do you believe that you can develop and improve with effort and perseverance?

06: UNDERSTANDING YOUR CURRENT MINDSET: A SELF-ASSESSMENT

– How do you view the success of others? Do you see it as a threat, or do you see it as an inspiration and motivator?

By answering these questions, you can gain insight into your current mindset. If you find that you have a fixed mindset, don't worry. The good news is that you can change your mindset and adopt a growth mindset. All it takes is a shift in your thoughts and beliefs.

In order to help you identify your current mindset, it is also helpful to reflect on past experiences and think about how you approached challenges and failures. This can give you a clearer picture of your thoughts and beliefs, and help you understand where you need to focus your efforts in order to shift to a growth mindset.

In conclusion, conducting a self-assessment is an important step in understanding your current mindset. By gaining insight into your thoughts and beliefs, you can begin the process of shifting to a growth mindset and unlock the power of positive thoughts and beliefs to transform your life.

07: Overcoming a Fixed Mindset: Strategies for Change

If you have a fixed mindset, it may feel difficult to change your thoughts and beliefs. However, with the right strategies, you can overcome a fixed mindset and adopt a growth mindset. Here are some strategies to help you make the shift:

— Reframe your thoughts: Start by becoming aware of your thoughts and beliefs. When you catch yourself thinking in a fixed mindset, try to reframe your thoughts in a more positive, growth-oriented way. For example, instead of saying "I'm not good at this," try saying "I'm still learning and improving."

— Embrace challenges: Instead of avoiding challenges, embrace them as opportunities for growth and development. Look at challenges as a chance to learn and improve, rather than as a threat to your abilities and skills.

— Seek out feedback: Seek out constructive criticism and feedback, and embrace it as a chance for growth and development. Ask others for feedback on your performance, and be open to constructive criticism.

07: OVERCOMING A FIXED MINDSET: STRATEGIES FOR CHANGE

– Celebrate failures: Instead of viewing failures as setbacks, view them as opportunities for learning and growth. Celebrate your failures and use them as a springboard for improvement.

– Surround yourself with growth-oriented people: Surround yourself with people who have a growth mindset and who are supportive and encouraging. Seek out mentors and role models who embody a growth mindset, and learn from them.

– Practice self-reflection: Take time to reflect on your thoughts and beliefs, and become more aware of your fixed mindset tendencies. Ask yourself what you can learn from failures and setbacks, and seek out opportunities for growth and development.

– Focus on the process, not just the outcome: Instead of focusing solely on the outcome, focus on the process of growth and development. Celebrate small victories along the way, and recognize the value of the journey, not just the destination.

In conclusion, overcoming a fixed mindset and adopting a

growth mindset takes time and effort. However, with the right strategies, you can make the shift and unlock the power of positive thoughts and beliefs to transform your life. Remember, it's never too late to start, and the benefits of a growth mindset are worth the effort.

08: The Role of Challenging Yourself in Developing a Growth Mindset

Challenging yourself is an important aspect of developing a growth mindset. By stepping outside of your comfort zone and taking on new challenges, you can foster personal growth and development, and cultivate a more positive, growth-oriented mindset. Here are some ways to challenge yourself:

– Set stretch goals: Set ambitious goals for yourself, and push yourself to reach them. This can help you build confidence and develop a growth mindset.

– Learn new skills: Take on new challenges and learn new skills. Whether it's learning a new language, trying a new hobby, or taking on a new project, expanding your skills and knowledge can help you develop a growth mindset.

– Collaborate with others: Work with others to tackle new challenges and projects. Collaborating with others can help you learn from others, and provide you with new perspectives and insights.

08: THE ROLE OF CHALLENGING YOURSELF IN DEVELOPING A GROWTH MINDSET

– Embrace uncertainty: Be open to new experiences and embrace uncertainty. This can help you become more comfortable with change and uncertainty, and foster a growth mindset.

– Take calculated risks: Take calculated risks and embrace new challenges. This can help you build resilience and develop a growth mindset.

– Celebrate your successes: Celebrate your successes and acknowledge your accomplishments, no matter how small they may be. This can help you build confidence and develop a growth mindset.

– Learn from your failures: When you face setbacks, take the time to reflect on what you can learn from them. This can help you build resilience and develop a growth mindset.

In conclusion, challenging yourself is an important aspect of developing a growth mindset. By embracing new challenges and pushing yourself outside of your comfort zone, you can cultivate a more positive, growth-oriented mindset and unlock the power of positive thoughts and beliefs to transform your life.

09: Embracing Failure as a Path to Growth and Success

In a fixed mindset, failure is seen as a negative outcome that reflects on one's abilities and worth. However, in a growth mindset, failure is viewed as an opportunity for growth and development. By embracing failure, you can unlock the full potential of a growth mindset and achieve greater success, happiness, and fulfillment. Here are some ways to embrace failure:

— Change your perspective: Start by changing your perspective on failure. Instead of viewing failure as a negative outcome, view it as a stepping stone on the path to success.

— Celebrate failures: Celebrate your failures and use them as a learning opportunity. Recognize that failures are an inevitable part of the learning and growth process.

— Reflect on failures: Take time to reflect on your failures and what you can learn from them. Ask yourself what went wrong, what you could have done differently, and what you can do better next time.

— Seek feedback: Seek feedback from others on your failures, and embrace it as a chance for growth and development. Ask others for their perspectives on what you could have done differently and what you can improve on.

– Learn from failures: Use failures as a learning opportunity, and apply what you have learned to future endeavors. Recognize that failures are an important part of the growth process, and embrace them as a path to growth and success.

– Don't dwell on failures: Don't dwell on your failures. Instead, focus on the present moment, and take action to move forward.

– Try again: Don't let failures discourage you. Instead, use them as motivation to try again, and approach new challenges with a growth mindset.

In conclusion, embracing failure is an important aspect of a growth mindset. By viewing failures as opportunities for growth and development, you can unlock the full potential of a growth mindset and achieve greater success, happiness, and fulfillment. Remember, it's not about avoiding failures, but about embracing them as a path to growth and success.

10: Understanding and Overcoming Negative Thoughts and Beliefs

Negative thoughts and beliefs can hold us back from achieving our full potential and living a fulfilling life. In order to cultivate a growth mindset and unlock the power of positive thoughts and beliefs, it's important to understand and overcome negative thoughts and beliefs. Here are some strategies to help you do just that:

– Identify negative thoughts: Start by identifying your negative thoughts and beliefs. Write them down and examine them closely. Ask yourself if these thoughts are based on fact or simply limiting beliefs.

– Challenge negative thoughts: Once you have identified your negative thoughts, challenge them. Ask yourself if they are truly accurate, and if not, reframe them into a more positive perspective.

– Replace negative thoughts: Replace negative thoughts with positive ones. Focus on your strengths, accomplishments, and positive experiences, and remind yourself of your worth and potential.

10: UNDERSTANDING AND OVERCOMING NEGATIVE THOUGHTS AND BELIEFS

– Practice mindfulness: Practice mindfulness and stay present in the moment. This can help you avoid negative thoughts and beliefs, and cultivate a more positive, growth-oriented mindset.

– Surround yourself with positive influences: Surround yourself with positive people, books, and media that support a growth mindset. This can help you stay motivated and avoid negative thoughts and beliefs.

– Engage in positive self-talk: Engage in positive self-talk, and focus on your strengths and potential. Remind yourself of your worth and what you have to offer.

– Practice gratitude: Practice gratitude and focus on the things you are thankful for in your life. This can help you cultivate a more positive, growth-oriented mindset.

In conclusion, understanding and overcoming negative thoughts and beliefs is an important aspect of developing a growth mindset. By focusing on positive thoughts and beliefs, and challenging and replacing negative thoughts, you can cultivate a more positive, growth-oriented mindset and unlock the power of positive thoughts and beliefs to transform your life.

11: Building a Positive Mindset: Strategies for Transformation

Adopting a positive, growth-oriented mindset can have a profound impact on your life, helping you achieve greater success, happiness, and fulfillment. Here are some strategies for building a positive mindset and transforming your thoughts:

— Cultivate gratitude: Practice gratitude regularly and focus on the things you are thankful for in your life. This can help you cultivate a more positive, growth-oriented mindset.

— Surround yourself with positivity: Surround yourself with positive people, books, and media that support a growth mindset. This can help you stay motivated and maintain a positive perspective.

— Practice self-reflection: Take time to reflect on your thoughts and beliefs, and identify any limiting beliefs that may be holding you back. Challenge these beliefs and reframe them into a more positive perspective.

— Embrace challenges: Embrace challenges as opportunities for growth and learning, and approach them with a growth mindset.

– Engage in positive self-talk: Engage in positive self-talk, and focus on your strengths and potential. Remind yourself of your worth and what you have to offer.

– Practice mindfulness: Practice mindfulness and stay present in the moment. This can help you cultivate a positive, growth-oriented mindset and avoid negative thoughts and beliefs.

– Set achievable goals: Set achievable goals for yourself, and focus on taking small steps towards your goals on a regular basis. Celebrate your progress and accomplishments, no matter how small.

– Focus on growth: Focus on growth and learning, rather than perfection or success. This can help you cultivate a growth mindset and approach challenges and setbacks with a positive perspective.

– Seek support: Seek support from friends, family, and mental health professionals, if necessary. Having a strong support system can help you maintain a positive, growth-oriented mindset and overcome any challenges that may arise.

In conclusion, building a positive mindset takes time and effort, but the benefits are well worth it. By focusing on positive thoughts and beliefs, embracing challenges, and seeking support, you can cultivate a positive, growth-oriented mindset and transform your thoughts, and ultimately your life.

12: The Power of Gratitude in Shaping Your Mindset

Gratitude is a powerful tool for shaping your mindset and transforming your thoughts. Here's how gratitude can help you cultivate a more positive, growth-oriented mindset:

— Increases positivity: Expressing gratitude can increase positive emotions, leading to greater overall well-being and happiness. It can help you focus on what you have, rather than what you lack, and improve your outlook on life.

— Reduces negativity: Regularly practicing gratitude can reduce negative thoughts and emotions, such as anger, frustration, and envy. This can help you avoid the pitfalls of a fixed mindset and maintain a positive outlook.

— Improves relationships: Gratitude can also improve your relationships by fostering positive emotions and increasing feelings of connection with others. When you focus on what you appreciate in others, you foster stronger relationships and build stronger bonds.

— Increases resilience: Gratitude can also increase resilience, helping you bounce back from challenges and setbacks with greater ease. By focusing on the positive aspects of your life, you can cultivate a growth mindset and avoid getting stuck in negative thoughts.

– Enhances motivation: Gratitude can also enhance motivation by increasing your sense of purpose and providing a sense of meaning. When you focus on what you are thankful for, you can cultivate a positive outlook and maintain a growth mindset, even in the face of challenges.

To cultivate gratitude in your life, consider implementing the following practices:

– Keep a gratitude journal: Write down things you are grateful for every day. This can help you focus on the positive aspects of your life and foster gratitude on a regular basis.

– Write thank-you notes: Write thank-you notes to people who have made a positive impact on your life. This can help you express your gratitude and build stronger relationships.

– Practice mindfulness: Practice mindfulness and stay present in the moment. This can help you cultivate gratit-

12: THE POWER OF GRATITUDE IN SHAPING YOUR MINDSET

ude by focusing on what is happening in the present moment and avoiding negative thoughts.

– Share gratitude with others: Share your gratitude with others and encourage them to share their own experiences of gratitude. This can help you foster a positive, growth-oriented mindset and spread positivity to others.

In conclusion, gratitude is a powerful tool for shaping your mindset and transforming your thoughts. By cultivating gratitude in your life, you can foster a positive outlook, increase resilience, and improve your relationships, leading to greater overall happiness and success.

13: Mindfulness: A Key Practice for Mindset Transformation

Mindfulness is a powerful practice that can help you transform your mindset and achieve greater success, happiness, and fulfillment. Here's how mindfulness can help you cultivate a growth mindset:

– Increases self-awareness: Mindfulness helps increase self-awareness by bringing your attention to the present moment and helping you observe your thoughts and emotions without judgment. This increased self-awareness can help you identify negative thought patterns and beliefs, and replace them with more positive, growth-oriented ones.

– Reduces stress: Mindfulness has been shown to reduce stress and improve overall well-being. By bringing your attention to the present moment, mindfulness can help you avoid getting caught up in worries and negative thoughts, leading to reduced stress and improved mental health.

– Improves focus: Mindfulness can also improve focus and concentration, helping you avoid distractions and stay on task. This increased focus can lead to greater productivity and success in all areas of life.

13: MINDFULNESS: A KEY PRACTICE FOR MINDSET TRANSFORMATION

– Increases resilience: Mindfulness can also increase resilience by helping you handle stress and challenges with greater ease. By bringing your attention to the present moment, mindfulness can help you avoid getting bogged down by negative thoughts and maintain a growth mindset in the face of adversity.

– Enhances emotional regulation: Mindfulness can also enhance emotional regulation by helping you manage your emotions and avoid being controlled by them. This increased emotional regulation can help you maintain a positive outlook and avoid negative thought patterns.

To incorporate mindfulness into your life, consider the following practices:

– Meditation: Regularly practice mindfulness meditation, which involves focusing on the present moment and observing your thoughts and emotions without judgment.

– Mindful breathing: Practice mindful breathing, which involves paying attention to your breath and using it as a tool to stay present in the moment.

13: MINDFULNESS: A KEY PRACTICE FOR MINDSET TRANSFORMATION

– Mindful movement: Incorporate mindful movement into your routine, such as yoga or tai chi, to increase mindfulness and reduce stress.

– Mindful observation: Practice mindful observation by paying attention to your surroundings and the present moment. This can help you avoid getting caught up in negative thoughts and maintain a growth mindset.

In conclusion, mindfulness is a powerful practice that can help you transform your mindset and achieve greater success, happiness, and fulfillment. By incorporating mindfulness into your life, you can increase self-awareness, reduce stress, improve focus, increase resilience, and enhance emotional regulation, leading to a more positive, growth-oriented mindset.

14: The Role of Mindset in Building Strong Relationships

Your mindset plays a significant role in the quality of your relationships, whether it be personal or professional. A growth mindset can help you build strong, healthy relationships, while a fixed mindset can limit your ability to connect with others. Here's how a growth mindset can impact your relationships:

— Improved communication: A growth mindset encourages open-mindedness and a willingness to understand other perspectives. This can lead to improved communication and a greater ability to resolve conflicts in a healthy manner.

— Increased empathy: A growth mindset also fosters empathy and a deeper understanding of others, which is essential for building strong relationships. By recognizing the challenges and experiences of others, you can form deeper connections and strengthen your relationships.

— Enhanced resilience: A growth mindset can also increase resilience in relationships, allowing you to handle challenges and conflicts with greater ease. This can lead to stronger relationships that are more likely to endure over time.

— Greater trust: A growth mindset also encourages trust, as it allows you to see the best in others and trust their intentions. This trust can lead to greater intimacy and a stronger bond between partners.

— Increased positivity: A growth mindset also fosters a positive outlook, which can have a significant impact on your relationships. By maintaining a positive attitude, you can help create a more harmonious and supportive environment, leading to stronger, healthier relationships.

To cultivate a growth mindset in your relationships, consider the following strategies:

— Practice active listening: When communicating with others, practice active listening to fully understand their perspective and build a deeper connection.

— Embrace challenges: Approach challenges in your relationships as opportunities for growth, rather than obstacles. This can help you handle conflicts with greater ease and strengthen your relationship.

14: THE ROLE OF MINDSET IN BUILDING STRONG RE-LATIONSHIPS

– Cultivate empathy: Practice empathy by putting yourself in others' shoes and recognizing their experiences and challenges. This can help you build deeper connections and strengthen your relationships.

– Foster positivity: Maintain a positive outlook and focus on the good in others, rather than dwelling on their flaws. This can help create a more harmonious and supportive environment in your relationships.

– Seek growth: Focus on growing and improving in your relationships, rather than maintaining the status quo. This can lead to greater intimacy and a stronger bond between partners.

In conclusion, a growth mindset plays a critical role in building strong relationships. By incorporating these strategies into your relationships, you can improve communication, increase empathy, enhance resilience, foster trust, and cultivate a positive outlook, leading to stronger, healthier relationships.

15: Mindset and Career Success: How to Reach Your Full Potential

Your mindset has a significant impact on your career success. A growth mindset can help you reach your full potential, while a fixed mindset can limit your ability to achieve success. Here's how a growth mindset can impact your career:

— Increased motivation: A growth mindset fosters a love of learning and a desire to improve, which can increase motivation and drive in your career.

— Improved resilience: A growth mindset also enhances resilience in the face of challenges, allowing you to handle setbacks and failures with greater ease. This can lead to greater success in the long run.

— Enhanced creativity: A growth mindset encourages creativity and out-of-the-box thinking, which can lead to new ideas and breakthroughs in your career.

— Greater opportunities: A growth mindset can also open up new opportunities by allowing you to see challenges as opportunities for growth and improvement.

15: MINDSET AND CAREER SUCCESS: HOW TO REACH YOUR FULL POTENTIAL

— Increased confidence: A growth mindset can also increase self-confidence, allowing you to take risks and pursue new opportunities with greater ease.

To cultivate a growth mindset in your career, consider the following strategies:

— Embrace challenges: Approach challenges in your career as opportunities for growth and improvement, rather than obstacles.

— Seek feedback: Seek out feedback and criticism to help identify areas for improvement and grow in your career.

— Learn continuously: Cultivate a love of learning and seek out new opportunities to develop your skills and knowledge.

— Take risks: Be willing to take risks and step outside your comfort zone to pursue new opportunities and reach your full potential.

— Focus on growth: Focus on growing and improving in your career, rather than simply maintaining the status quo.

In conclusion, a growth mindset plays a critical role in career success. By incorporating these strategies into your career, you can increase motivation, enhance resilience, improve creativity, open up new opportunities, and increase self-confidence, leading to greater success and fulfillment in your career.

16: Mindset and Financial Abundance: Achieving Your Financial Goals

Your mindset can have a profound impact on your financial situation. A fixed mindset can lead to limiting beliefs and behaviors that can hold you back from achieving financial abundance, while a growth mindset can help you achieve your financial goals. Here's how a growth mindset can impact your financial situation:

— Increased motivation: A growth mindset fosters a love of learning and a desire to improve, which can increase motivation and drive in pursuing financial goals.

— Improved decision-making: A growth mindset can also lead to improved decision-making, allowing you to make smart financial choices and avoid costly mistakes.

— Enhanced creativity: A growth mindset encourages creativity and out-of-the-box thinking, which can lead to new ideas for generating income and wealth.

— Greater opportunities: A growth mindset can also open up new opportunities for financial growth, by allowing you to see challenges as opportunities for improvement.

– Increased confidence: A growth mindset can also increase self-confidence, allowing you to take risks and pursue new financial opportunities with greater ease.

To cultivate a growth mindset in your finances, consider the following strategies:

– Embrace challenges: Approach financial challenges as opportunities for growth and improvement, rather than obstacles.

– Seek knowledge: Seek out knowledge and information to help you make informed financial decisions and reach your goals.

– Take action: Take action and take control of your finances, rather than simply waiting for things to happen.

– Invest in yourself: Invest in yourself and your financial education, to help you achieve financial abundance in the long run.

– Focus on growth: Focus on growing and improving your

financial situation, rather than simply maintaining the status quo.

In conclusion, a growth mindset plays a critical role in financial abundance. By incorporating these strategies into your finances, you can increase motivation, improve decision-making, enhance creativity, open up new opportunities, and increase self-confidence, leading to greater financial success and fulfillment.

17: The Mindset of a Champion: How to Win in Life and Business

Chapter 17: The Mindset of a Champion: How to Win in Life and Business

Champions are not born, they are made. A champion mindset is the result of developing the right attitude and habits that enable you to succeed in life and business. Whether you're pursuing a personal goal or striving for success in your career, the mindset of a champion can help you reach your full potential.

— A growth mindset: The foundation of the champion mindset is a growth mindset, which is the belief that you can improve and achieve your goals through effort and hard work.

— Positive attitude: Champions have a positive attitude and an optimistic outlook, which helps them overcome obstacles and keep moving forward.

— Focus: Champions are highly focused and driven, and they use their focus to achieve their goals and stay on track.

— Resilience: Champions are resilient and able to bounce back from setbacks and failures, which allows them to keep pushing forward and achieving their goals.

– Confidence: Champions have confidence in themselves and their abilities, which allows them to take risks and seize opportunities.

To develop the mindset of a champion, consider the following strategies:

– Embrace failure: Embrace failure as a learning opportunity and a stepping stone to success.

– Surround yourself with positive influences: Surround yourself with positive people and influences that support and inspire you.

– Stay focused on your goals: Stay focused on your goals and maintain a clear vision of what you want to achieve.

– Cultivate resilience: Cultivate resilience by facing challenges and setbacks head-on, and using them as opportunities for growth.

– Believe in yourself: Believe in yourself and your abilities, and have confidence in your capacity to achieve your goals.

17: THE MINDSET OF A CHAMPION: HOW TO WIN IN LIFE AND BUSINESS

In conclusion, the mindset of a champion is a combination of a growth mindset, positive attitude, focus, resilience, and confidence. By adopting these principles and habits, you can develop the mindset of a champion, and achieve greater success, happiness, and fulfillment in life and business.

18: Mindset and Creativity: Unleashing Your Inner Genius

Creativity is a vital part of human life and is essential for personal and professional success. Whether you are an artist, a writer, an entrepreneur, or simply someone who wants to live a fulfilling life, a growth mindset can help you unleash your inner genius and tap into your full creative potential.

— Define creativity: Creativity is the ability to generate new and unique ideas and turn them into reality.

— The connection between mindset and creativity: A growth mindset is essential for unlocking creativity because it enables you to embrace challenges and failures as opportunities for growth and learning.

— Overcoming creative blocks: With a growth mindset, you can overcome creative blocks and limitations by embracing challenges and failures and using them as opportunities to grow and develop new skills.

— Embracing experimentation: Creativity requires experimentation and the willingness to take risks. With a growth mindset, you can embrace experimentation and take risks, knowing that failure is simply a stepping stone to success.

– Encouraging a creative environment: Encouraging a creative environment by surrounding yourself with positive people and influences, and by engaging in activities and hobbies that inspire and energize you.

To unleash your inner genius and tap into your full creative potential, consider the following strategies:

– Cultivate a growth mindset: Cultivate a growth mindset by embracing challenges and failures as opportunities for growth and learning, and by having an optimistic outlook and a positive attitude.

– Embrace experimentation: Embrace experimentation and take risks, knowing that failure is simply a stepping stone to success.

– Surround yourself with positive influences: Surround yourself with positive people and influences that support and inspire you.

– Engage in activities that inspire and energize you: Engage

in activities and hobbies that inspire and energize you, and
that tap into your natural talents and passions.

– Keep learning and growing: Keep learning and growing by
engaging in new experiences and taking on new challenges,
and by continuously expanding your skills and knowledge.

In conclusion, a growth mindset is essential for unlocking
creativity and unleashing your inner genius. By embracing
challenges and failures as opportunities for growth, embracing experimentation, surrounding yourself with positive
influences, engaging in activities that inspire you, and continuously learning and growing, you can tap into your full
creative potential and achieve greater success, happiness,
and fulfillment.

19: The Mindset of Leadership: Achieving Greatness Through Positive Thinking

Leadership is an important aspect of life, whether you are a manager, an entrepreneur, a coach, or simply someone who wants to make a positive impact in your community. A growth mindset is essential for becoming an effective leader, as it enables you to tap into your full potential and achieve greatness through positive thinking and action.

The role of mindset in leadership: Your mindset plays a critical role in your ability to lead and inspire others, as it shapes your perception of yourself, others, and the world around you.

– The benefits of a growth mindset for leaders: With a growth mindset, leaders are better equipped to face challenges, embrace change, and continuously improve and innovate. They are also better able to build strong relationships, create a positive work environment, and foster a culture of growth and learning.

– Overcoming the challenges of leadership: Leadership can be challenging, but with a growth mindset, leaders can overcome obstacles and challenges by viewing them as opportunities for growth and learning.

— Inspiring and empowering others: With a growth mindset, leaders are better able to inspire and empower others, by creating a positive and supportive work environment, and by promoting growth, learning, and innovation.

— Building a legacy of leadership: With a growth mindset, leaders can build a legacy of leadership that inspires and motivates others, and that leaves a lasting impact on the world.

To develop a growth mindset and achieve greatness as a leader, consider the following strategies:

— Embrace challenges and failures as opportunities for growth and learning: Embrace challenges and failures as opportunities for growth and learning, and use them to continuously improve and innovate.

— Build strong relationships: Build strong relationships with your team, colleagues, and stakeholders by being open, honest, and supportive.

19: THE MINDSET OF LEADERSHIP: ACHIEVING GREATNESS THROUGH POSITIVE THINKING

– Create a positive work environment: Create a positive work environment by fostering a culture of growth, learning, and innovation, and by encouraging and empowering others.

– Lead by example: Lead by example by demonstrating a positive attitude and a commitment to growth and learning.

– Continuously improve and innovate: Continuously improve and innovate by embracing new ideas, experimenting with new approaches, and staying up-to-date with the latest trends and best practices in leadership.

In conclusion, a growth mindset is essential for achieving greatness as a leader. By embracing challenges and failures as opportunities for growth, building strong relationships, creating a positive work environment, leading by example, and continuously improving and innovating, you can tap into your full potential and make a positive impact in your community.

20: Mindset and Health: The Connection Between Thoughts and Physical Well-Being

Your mindset has a profound impact on your physical health. The thoughts you have about yourself, your body, and your health can either support or hinder your efforts to maintain good health.

Positive thoughts and beliefs about health can boost your immune system, reduce stress, and improve your overall well-being. On the other hand, negative thoughts and beliefs can lead to stress, anxiety, and depression, which can take a toll on your physical health.

Studies have shown that people with a positive mindset are more likely to lead a healthy lifestyle. They are more likely to eat well, exercise regularly, and manage stress effectively. They also have a better outlook on life, which can boost their overall health and happiness.

In contrast, people with a negative mindset tend to engage in unhealthy behaviors such as overeating, smoking, and neglecting their physical health. They also tend to have a more negative outlook on life, which can impact their mental and physical health.

The good news is that you can change your mindset and, as a result, improve your health. You can start by paying attention to the thoughts you have about yourself and your health. Challenge any negative thoughts or beliefs you may have and replace them with positive, empowering ones.

Incorporating mindfulness into your daily routine can also help you cultivate a positive mindset. Mindfulness is the practice of focusing your attention on the present moment, without judgment. It can help you become more aware of your thoughts and beliefs and help you develop a healthier outlook on life.

Exercise is also a great way to improve your mindset and physical health. Exercise releases endorphins, the feel-good hormone, which can help boost your mood and reduce stress. It can also help you build a stronger, healthier body, which can improve your overall health and well-being.

In conclusion, your mindset has a profound impact on your physical health. By developing a positive mindset, you can improve your overall well-being and lead a healthier, happier life.

21: The Mindset of the Entrepreneur: Turning Your Dreams into Reality

Entrepreneurship is not just about starting a business, it's about having a mindset that is focused on creating value, solving problems, and embracing risk and uncertainty. A growth mindset is essential for anyone looking to start their own business, as it provides the resilience, perseverance, and adaptability needed to succeed.

One of the key traits of an entrepreneurial mindset is a strong sense of self-belief. Entrepreneurs must believe in their ideas and their abilities to bring those ideas to life. They must also have a strong sense of purpose, which drives them to create something meaningful and impactful.

Another key aspect of the entrepreneurial mindset is an openness to learning and growth. Entrepreneurs must be willing to take risks, try new things, and be comfortable with failure. They must also be willing to continuously improve, evolve their ideas, and pivot as needed.

Having a growth mindset also means embracing a growth-oriented approach to challenges and setbacks. Instead of viewing them as insurmountable obstacles, entrepreneurs see them as opportunities for learning and growth. This mindset allows entrepreneurs to overcome the challenges they face and turn their failures into opportunities for growth and success.

One of the most important traits of an entrepreneurial mindset is the ability to turn ideas into action. Entrepreneurs must have a bias towards action, a willingness to take the first step, and a drive to bring their ideas to life. This requires a level of creativity, resourcefulness, and determination that is essential for success.

Another important aspect of the entrepreneurial mindset is the ability to build and manage relationships. Entrepreneurs must have strong communication and interpersonal skills, and be able to build trust and credibility with potential partners, customers, and investors. They must also be able to surround themselves with a talented team that can help bring their vision to life.

In conclusion, the entrepreneurial mindset is a combination of self-belief, a growth-oriented approach, a bias towards action, and the ability to build and manage relationships. By

adopting these traits, you can turn your dreams into reality
and achieve success as an entrepreneur.

22: The Mindset of a Learner: A Lifetime of Growth and Development

The mindset of a learner is one of the most important traits you can develop in your life. By adopting a growth mindset and embracing a love of learning, you can continue to grow, develop, and achieve new levels of success and fulfillment.

The first step in developing a learner's mindset is to adopt a growth-oriented approach to education and learning. This means seeing challenges as opportunities for growth and improvement, and embracing the process of learning, even when it's difficult or uncomfortable.

One of the benefits of a learner's mindset is that it helps you stay curious and engaged with the world around you. By seeking out new knowledge and experiences, you can continue to expand your horizons and broaden your perspective.

Another important aspect of a learner's mindset is the ability to learn from failure. By embracing failure as a learning opportunity, you can gain valuable insights into what works and what doesn't, and use that knowledge to inform future decision making.

In order to develop a learner's mindset, it's also important to adopt a continuous improvement mentality. This means seeking out new learning opportunities, setting goals for personal growth, and actively working to improve in areas that are important to you.

In addition to personal growth, a learner's mindset can also help you develop stronger relationships with others. By being open and curious, you can build better connections with those around you, and gain new perspectives and insights.

Finally, a learner's mindset can help you achieve greater success in your career. By embracing continuous learning and development, you can build the skills and knowledge needed to succeed in your field, and continuously grow and advance in your career.

In conclusion, the mindset of a learner is a powerful tool for growth and development. By embracing a love of learning and a growth-oriented approach, you can continue to grow, improve, and achieve new levels of success and fulfillment in your life.

23: Mindset and Resilience: Overcoming Adversity and Hardship

Adversity is a part of life, and how we choose to approach it can greatly impact our well-being and success. Those with a fixed mindset may view challenges as threats to their self-esteem, leading to feelings of helplessness and hopelessness. On the other hand, those with a growth mindset view challenges as opportunities for growth and improvement.

The connection between mindset and resilience is crucial, as resilience is the ability to bounce back from adversity. A growth mindset can help us build resilience by teaching us to embrace challenges, seek out support, and see setbacks as opportunities for growth. This kind of resilience is key to overcoming adversity and hardship.

In this chapter, we will explore the following topics:

— The relationship between mindset and resilience

— How a growth mindset can help you build resilience

— Strategies for overcoming adversity and hardship

— The importance of self-care in developing resilience

23: MINDSET AND RESILIENCE: OVERCOMING ADVERSITY AND HARDSHIP

— The role of positive thinking in building resilience

— The impact of resilience on overall well-being and success

Building resilience is a process, and it takes time and effort. However, with a growth mindset and the right strategies, anyone can become more resilient and better equipped to handle the challenges that life throws their way.

One of the most important steps in building resilience is developing a growth mindset. A growth mindset allows you to see challenges as opportunities for growth and improvement, and it helps you to believe in your own abilities to overcome adversity. This mindset also helps you to view setbacks as temporary and to focus on the long-term.

Another key strategy for building resilience is seeking out support. This can be from friends, family, or a therapist, but it's important to have a support system in place when times are tough. Additionally, it's important to engage in self-care practices like exercise, healthy eating, and mindfulness to help maintain your physical and mental well-being.

Finally, practicing positive thinking can also help you to

build resilience. This involves focusing on the good in any situation, and looking for the silver lining in tough times. It also involves reframing negative thoughts and beliefs, and replacing them with positive, empowering ones.

In conclusion, resilience is an important aspect of a growth mindset, and it's a crucial tool for overcoming adversity and hardship. By developing a growth mindset, seeking out support, engaging in self-care practices, and practicing positive thinking, you can build resilience and become better equipped to handle life's challenges.

24: Mindset and Happiness: Achieving Lasting Joy and Fulfillment

Happiness is a feeling that most people strive for, yet many struggle to attain. However, research has shown that our mindset plays a significant role in our level of happiness and well-being. In this chapter, we will explore the connection between mindset and happiness, and how a growth mindset can help us achieve greater joy and fulfillment in life.

A fixed mindset can limit our happiness by causing us to focus on external validation, and compare ourselves to others. This can lead to feelings of inadequacy and a fear of failure, which can undermine our confidence and limit our ability to pursue the things that bring us happiness. On the other hand, a growth mindset allows us to focus on our own personal growth and development, and embrace challenges as opportunities for growth.

One of the key benefits of adopting a growth mindset is that it helps us cultivate a more positive outlook on life. A positive outlook can lead to increased feelings of joy, satisfaction, and fulfillment, and can help us build stronger relationships and more meaningful connections with others. It can also help us maintain a sense of resilience in the face of adversity, which is crucial for long-term happiness.

In addition to fostering a positive outlook, a growth mindset can also help us develop a greater sense of gratitude. When we adopt a growth mindset, we tend to focus on the things we have rather than what we lack. This shift in perspective can help us feel more grateful for what we have and increase our sense of happiness and well-being.

Mindfulness is another key practice for fostering happiness and well-being. Mindfulness involves paying attention to the present moment, without judgment, and can help us cultivate a greater sense of inner peace and contentment. Regular mindfulness practice can also help us develop a greater capacity for compassion, empathy, and understanding, which can improve our relationships and enhance our overall sense of happiness and fulfillment.

In conclusion, adopting a growth mindset is essential for achieving lasting happiness and fulfillment in life. By focusing on our own growth and development, cultivating a positive outlook, and embracing mindfulness, we can tap into the power of our thoughts to transform our lives and achieve greater success, happiness, and fulfillment.

25: The Mindset of a Problem Solver: Finding Solutions and Overcoming Obstacles

One of the most important aspects of developing a growth mindset is the ability to solve problems effectively. A problem-solving mindset is crucial for success in both personal and professional life. In this chapter, we will explore how to develop a problem-solving mindset and how it can help you overcome obstacles and find solutions to life's challenges.

A problem-solving mindset involves approaching challenges with a positive attitude and an open mind. It requires a willingness to try new things, take risks, and be flexible in your thinking. People with a problem-solving mindset are able to think creatively and come up with innovative solutions to problems. They are not afraid of failure, but see it as an opportunity to learn and grow.

One key aspect of a problem-solving mindset is the ability to think critically. This means looking at problems from multiple angles and considering different possible solutions. It also involves being able to analyze information, weigh the pros and cons of different options, and make decisions based on that information.

Another important aspect of a problem-solving mindset is persistence. This means continuing to work on a problem even when it seems difficult or impossible to solve. A problem-solver doesn't give up easily, but instead keeps trying different approaches until they find a solution that works.

Developing a problem-solving mindset can be challenging, but it is well worth the effort. By becoming a better problem-solver, you will be able to overcome obstacles and achieve your goals more effectively. You will also become more confident and resilient, as you will know that you have the skills and determination to handle any challenges that come your way.

Here are some strategies for developing a problem-solving mindset:

– Practice thinking critically. Try to approach problems from different angles and consider multiple possible solutions.

– Seek out new challenges. By taking on new challenges,

you will be forced to think creatively and develop your problem-solving skills.

– Embrace failure. Instead of seeing failure as a negative, try to see it as an opportunity to learn and grow.

– Surround yourself with positive, supportive people. Having a supportive network can help you stay motivated and optimistic as you work to solve problems.

– Focus on solutions, not problems. Instead of dwelling on the difficulties you face, try to focus on finding solutions and taking action.

By adopting a problem-solving mindset, you will be able to overcome obstacles and achieve greater success, happiness, and fulfillment in your life. So start today by focusing on developing your problem-solving skills and embracing a positive, growth-oriented approach to life's challenges.

26: The Mindset of a Goal-Setter: Achieving Your Dreams and Aspirations

Setting and achieving goals is a vital part of personal and professional success. But what sets apart those who successfully reach their goals from those who struggle? The answer lies in mindset. A growth mindset allows you to approach goal-setting with a positive and proactive attitude, making it easier to overcome obstacles and turn your aspirations into realities.

The first step in becoming a goal-setter is to understand what it means to have a growth mindset. People with a growth mindset believe in their ability to grow and develop through hard work and dedication. They understand that challenges are opportunities for growth, and that setbacks are temporary rather than permanent.

Having a growth mindset when it comes to goal-setting means embracing challenges and embracing the journey towards reaching your goals. It means not being discouraged by setbacks and instead using them as opportunities to learn and grow. It means being open-minded and flexible, willing to adjust your goals and strategies as you go along.

In order to cultivate a growth mindset when it comes to goal-setting, it's important to focus on the process rather than just the end result. Celebrate each small step forward, acknowledge your progress, and focus on what you've learned along the way. This will help you stay motivated and keep moving towards your goals, even when the going gets tough.

Another key aspect of the mindset of a goal-setter is taking personal responsibility for your goals and the steps you take to reach them. This means being proactive and taking own-ership of your progress, rather than waiting for someone else to help you or waiting for opportunities to fall into your lap.

It's also important to have a growth mindset when it comes to the goals you set for yourself. Rather than focusing on the end result, focus on the growth and learning that you will experience along the way. This will help you stay motivated and keep pushing yourself forward, even when the path to your goal is challenging.

26: THE MINDSET OF A GOAL-SETTER: ACHIEVING YOUR DREAMS AND ASPIRATIONS

Finally, to cultivate the mindset of a goal-setter, it's important to surround yourself with positive and supportive people. Surround yourself with people who believe in you and your goals, and who will encourage and support you along the way. This will help you stay focused and motivated, and will give you the strength and support you need to overcome any obstacles that arise.

In conclusion, the mindset of a goal-setter is crucial to achieving your dreams and aspirations. By embracing a growth mindset, taking personal responsibility for your progress, and focusing on the journey rather than just the end result, you can set and achieve your goals with confidence and success.

27: Mindset and Personal Growth: A Journey to Self-Discovery

Personal growth is a lifelong journey that requires a growth mindset. Your mindset shapes how you approach challenges and opportunities, and it determines whether you see the world as a place full of possibilities or one that limits you. To reach your full potential and achieve your goals, it's important to adopt a growth mindset.

The first step in personal growth is to understand your current mindset. Take some time to reflect on your thoughts, beliefs, and behaviors. Are you open to new ideas and experiences? Do you embrace change? Are you motivated by challenges? If your answer to these questions is yes, then you likely have a growth mindset. However, if you tend to avoid challenges, feel threatened by change, and cling to familiar ways of thinking, you may have a fixed mindset.

To develop a growth mindset, you need to challenge your limiting beliefs and negative thoughts. Start by recognizing your strengths and areas for improvement. Focus on what you can control, rather than what you can't. Embrace challenges and see them as opportunities to grow, rather than as threats. Celebrate your successes, no matter how small they are, and learn from your failures.

Another important aspect of personal growth is mindful-ness. Practicing mindfulness can help you cultivate a growth mindset by bringing your focus to the present moment. When you're mindful, you're more aware of your thoughts, feelings, and sensations, and you can respond to them with compassion and wisdom. This awareness can help you identify and challenge negative thoughts and beliefs that limit your growth.

Finally, personal growth requires a willingness to be vulner-able and take risks. To grow, you need to step outside your comfort zone, try new things, and expose yourself to new experiences. You may experience failures and setbacks along the way, but it's important to see these as opportunit-ies to learn and grow, rather than as reasons to give up.

In conclusion, adopting a growth mindset is key to personal growth and self-discovery. By embracing challenges, practi-cing mindfulness, and taking risks, you can tap into your full potential and achieve your dreams. By developing a growth mindset, you can transform your thoughts, trans-form your life, and experience greater success, happiness, and fulfillment.

28: Mindset and Spirituality: Achieving Inner Peace and Harmony

The connection between mindset and spirituality is undeniable. A person's outlook on life and the world around them can have a profound impact on their sense of purpose, peace, and fulfillment. This chapter explores the intersection between spirituality and mindset, and the impact that adopting a growth mindset can have on one's spiritual journey.

The concept of spirituality can be difficult to define, as it can mean different things to different people. Some see spirituality as a connection to a higher power or divine force, while others see it as a sense of inner peace and connectedness to all living things. Regardless of how one defines spirituality, it is an integral part of many people's lives, providing a sense of meaning and purpose in the midst of life's challenges and hardships.

A growth mindset is characterized by an openness to new experiences, a willingness to learn and grow, and a focus on personal development. When combined with spirituality, this type of mindset can lead to greater inner peace, happiness, and a deeper sense of purpose. Those who adopt a growth mindset are more likely to be open to new spiritual experiences, to embrace growth and change, and to seek out opportunities for personal development.

One of the key benefits of adopting a growth mindset in the realm of spirituality is the ability to overcome challenges and setbacks. Those with a growth mindset are more likely to see difficulties as opportunities for growth, rather than as obstacles to be overcome. They are also more likely to be resilient in the face of adversity, and to use their spiritual beliefs and practices to help them stay focused and centered in the midst of difficult times.

In addition, a growth mindset can help individuals to cultivate a deeper sense of inner peace and harmony. By focusing on personal development and growth, individuals can learn to let go of negative thoughts and beliefs, and to cultivate a sense of gratitude and contentment. This, in turn, can help them to develop a more positive outlook on life, and to find meaning and purpose in even the most challenging of circumstances.

28: MINDSET AND SPIRITUALITY: ACHIEVING INNER PEACE AND HARMONY

Ultimately, the intersection between mindset and spirituality can be a powerful force for personal growth and transformation. By embracing a growth mindset, individuals can tap into their full spiritual potential, and achieve a greater sense of peace, happiness, and fulfillment. Whether through meditation, mindfulness, or other spiritual practices, adopting a growth mindset can help individuals to achieve greater spiritual growth and development, and to experience a deeper sense of connection to the world around them.

29: The Mindset of a Giver: Living a Life of Service and Generosity

The concept of giving is an integral part of personal growth and happiness. Giving is an act of kindness, generosity, and selflessness that has the power to transform not only the lives of others but also our own. In this chapter, we will explore the mindset of a giver and the positive impact it has on our lives.

A giver's mindset is centered around the belief that we can make a difference in the world by giving our time, resources, and support to those in need. This mindset encourages us to focus on the needs of others and to look for opportunities to serve and help those around us. When we adopt this mindset, we become more aware of the opportunities to make a positive impact and more motivated to take action.

The benefits of adopting a giver's mindset are numerous. Research has shown that giving increases feelings of happiness, reduces stress and anxiety, and improves our physical health. Furthermore, it helps to build strong relationships, create a sense of community, and foster a greater sense of purpose in our lives.

29: THE MINDSET OF A GIVER: LIVING A LIFE OF SERVICE AND GENEROSITY

When we adopt the mindset of a giver, we become more confident, resilient, and optimistic. This mindset helps us to overcome adversity and to see challenges as opportunities for growth and learning. Furthermore, it helps us to cultivate a positive and optimistic outlook on life, which in turn, contributes to our overall well-being.

In order to cultivate a giver's mindset, it is important to focus on the joy and fulfillment that giving brings, rather than the financial or material rewards. It is also important to find ways to give back that align with our values, interests, and passions. Whether it be volunteering at a local non-profit organization, mentoring a young person, or simply helping a neighbor in need, there are many opportunities to give back and make a difference.

In conclusion, the mindset of a giver is an essential component of personal growth and happiness. By embracing this mindset, we can enrich our lives and the lives of others. When we give of ourselves, we create a ripple effect that has the power to transform the world. So, embrace the mindset of a giver, and start making a positive impact today!

30: Mindset and the Environment: How Your Thoughts Affect the World Around You

The environment plays a crucial role in shaping our lives and wellbeing, and it is up to us to ensure that it remains healthy and sustainable for future generations. Our mindset has a profound impact on how we view the world and how we interact with our surroundings. A negative and apathetic mindset can lead to careless behavior, neglect, and destruction of the environment, whereas a positive and proactive mindset can foster a sense of stewardship and conservation.

It has been shown that people who view themselves as environmentally responsible tend to have more pro-environmental attitudes and behaviors. These individuals are more likely to recycle, conserve energy, reduce waste, and take an active role in environmental activism. This is because they understand the importance of the environment and are motivated to make a positive impact.

In contrast, people who have a fixed mindset may view environmental issues as too complex or overwhelming to tackle. They may dismiss environmental concerns as irrelevant to their daily lives and feel that their individual actions cannot make a difference. This can lead to a lack of engagement and inaction, which contributes to environmental degradation.

To develop a positive and proactive mindset towards the environment, it is essential to understand the interconnectedness of all living things and to recognize that our actions have a direct impact on the environment. This requires a shift in perspective and a willingness to challenge our beliefs and behaviors.

Here are some strategies for developing a positive and environmentally conscious mindset:

– Cultivate a sense of awe and wonder for the natural world. Take time to observe and appreciate the beauty and diversity of the environment.

– Educate yourself about environmental issues. Read books, watch documentaries, and attend seminars to increase your knowledge and understanding of the environment.

– Surround yourself with people who share your values.

30: MINDSET AND THE ENVIRONMENT: HOW YOUR THOUGHTS AFFECT THE WORLD AROUND YOU

Join environmental groups, attend environmental events, and participate in environmental activism.

– Make environmentally conscious choices. Reduce your carbon footprint, conserve energy, recycle, and use environmentally friendly products.

– Practice mindfulness and gratitude. Take time to reflect on the environment and appreciate its beauty and value.

By adopting a positive and proactive mindset towards the environment, we can create a world that is healthier, more sustainable, and more harmonious for all living things. We have the power to shape our thoughts, attitudes, and behaviors, and to create a positive impact on the world around us.

31: The Mindset of Success: Achieving Your Goals and Dreams

Success is a journey, not a destination, and your mindset is the key that opens the door to unlimited opportunities and possibilities. A positive, growth-oriented mindset can help you achieve greater success in all areas of your life, from your career and finances to your relationships and personal growth. In this chapter, we will explore the mindset of success and how it can help you reach your full potential.

To start, let's define what success means to you. Success can mean different things to different people. For some, it might be financial wealth and material possessions, while for others, it might be personal fulfillment and happiness. No matter what success means to you, having a positive and growth-oriented mindset is essential to reaching your goals.

One of the key elements of the mindset of success is a belief in yourself and your abilities. When you have confidence in yourself and your abilities, you are more likely to take risks and try new things, which are essential steps in achieving your goals. Confidence also allows you to handle setbacks and failures with resilience and determination, knowing that you have the skills and resources to overcome any obstacle.

Another important aspect of the mindset of success is a positive attitude. When you adopt a positive outlook, you are more likely to see opportunities and possibilities in every situation, rather than focusing on the negatives. This mindset shift can be transformational, helping you to tackle challenges with confidence and optimism, and to overcome obstacles more easily.

In addition to a belief in yourself and a positive attitude, the mindset of success also involves a willingness to learn and grow. Successful people are constantly learning and growing, always seeking out new information and new experiences to expand their knowledge and skills. This approach to life keeps you open to new possibilities and helps you to stay on track as you work towards your goals.

Finally, the mindset of success requires a clear vision of what you want to achieve and a plan for how you will get there. When you have a clear understanding of your goals and a plan for how to achieve them, you are more likely to stay focused and motivated, and to experience greater success in your journey.

31: THE MINDSET OF SUCCESS: ACHIEVING YOUR GOALS AND DREAMS

In conclusion, the mindset of success is a powerful tool that can help you achieve greater success, happiness, and fulfillment in all areas of your life. By embracing a growth-oriented mindset, believing in yourself and your abilities, adopting a positive attitude, learning and growing, and having a clear vision and plan, you can unlock the power of your thoughts and transform your life.

32: Mindset and Positive Thinking: The Path to a Better Life

Positive thinking is a powerful tool that can help transform your life. With the right mindset, you can overcome challenges, achieve your goals, and experience greater happiness and fulfillment. In this chapter, we will explore the relationship between mindset and positive thinking, and how you can develop a more positive outlook on life.

First, let's define what is meant by positive thinking. Positive thinking refers to an optimistic and hopeful mindset that focuses on the good things in life. It involves looking for the best in every situation, focusing on solutions rather than problems, and seeing challenges as opportunities for growth and development.

Positive thinking has been shown to have numerous benefits for both mental and physical health. Research has found that individuals with a positive outlook are more likely to experience greater happiness, better physical health, and longer lifespan. They are also less likely to experience stress, anxiety, and depression.

One of the keys to developing a positive mindset is to surround yourself with positive influences. This includes surrounding yourself with positive people, engaging in positive activities, and avoiding negative thoughts and behaviors. Additionally, it is important to engage in positive self-talk and to focus on what you are grateful for in your life.

Another key component to developing a positive mindset is to practice mindfulness. Mindfulness is the practice of being fully present and aware in the moment, without judgment. It has been shown to reduce stress, improve mental clarity, and increase positive thinking.

Finally, it is important to recognize that positive thinking is a habit that can be developed over time. Just like any other habit, it requires consistent practice and effort to become part of your daily routine. This means making a conscious effort to focus on the positive, and to engage in practices that support positive thinking.

In conclusion, the relationship between mindset and positive thinking is crucial for achieving success, happiness, and fulfillment. By developing a positive mindset, you can unlock the power of positive thinking, and create a life filled with joy, peace, and prosperity.

33: Mindset and the Law of Attraction: Attracting What You Want in Life

The Law of Attraction is a popular concept that states that you can attract positive experiences and outcomes into your life through the power of your thoughts and beliefs. This principle is based on the idea that like attracts like, and that what you focus on, you will bring into your life.

There is a strong connection between your mindset and the Law of Attraction, as your thoughts and beliefs can either attract positive experiences or repel them. If you have a growth mindset, you are likely to focus on positive thoughts and beliefs that will help you attract what you want in life. On the other hand, if you have a fixed mindset, you may focus on negative thoughts and beliefs that will repel what you want.

One of the key principles of the Law of Attraction is to focus on what you want, rather than what you don't want. When you focus on what you want, you send a clear message to the universe, and it responds by bringing it into your life. This can be done through visualization, affirmations, and other techniques that help you align your thoughts and beliefs with your desires.

It's important to note that the Law of Attraction is not a magic formula that will make all your dreams come true instantly. Instead, it's a process that requires time, effort, and persistence. However, if you can adopt a growth mindset and focus on positive thoughts and beliefs, you can increase your chances of attracting what you want into your life.

One of the benefits of incorporating the Law of Attraction into your mindset is that it can help you develop a more positive and optimistic outlook on life. This, in turn, can help you attract more positive experiences, relationships, and opportunities. It can also help you overcome obstacles and challenges, as you will be able to see them as opportunities for growth, rather than insurmountable problems.

In conclusion, the connection between mindset and the Law of Attraction is strong, as your thoughts and beliefs can either attract or repel what you want in life. By incorporating the principles of the Law of Attraction into your mindset, you can increase your chances of attracting positive experiences, relationships, and opportunities into your life, and achieve greater success, happiness, and fulfillment.

34: Mindset and Forgiveness: The Key to Inner Peace and Happiness

Forgiveness is an essential aspect of personal growth and development, and it is closely tied to our mindset. Our mindset shapes our attitudes, beliefs, and behaviors, and it greatly affects our ability to forgive others and ourselves. A growth mindset, characterized by a belief in personal growth, resilience, and the ability to change, can help us to cultivate a spirit of forgiveness and compassion.

The benefits of forgiveness are numerous and well-documented. Forgiving others can reduce feelings of anger and resentment, improve relationships, and promote feelings of peace and well-being. Forgiving ourselves can also be beneficial, helping us to overcome feelings of guilt, shame, and self-blame. Additionally, forgiveness can lead to greater empathy and understanding, allowing us to connect more deeply with others and to build stronger relationships.

However, the road to forgiveness can be challenging, especially for those with a fixed mindset, who may view forgiveness as weakness or as an admission of defeat. This can make it difficult to let go of negative feelings and to move on from past hurt. The good news is that forgiveness is a skill that can be developed and cultivated with practice.

To develop a mindset of forgiveness, it is important to understand that forgiveness is not condoning bad behavior or forgetting about past hurt. Instead, it is about letting go of negative emotions, such as anger and resentment, and embracing a more positive and compassionate outlook.

One way to cultivate a spirit of forgiveness is through mindfulness practices, such as meditation and deep breathing. These practices can help to calm the mind and reduce feelings of stress and anxiety, making it easier to let go of negative emotions and to embrace a more positive outlook.

Another strategy for developing a mindset of forgiveness is to engage in self-reflection and to work on changing negative thought patterns. This may involve questioning our assumptions and beliefs about forgiveness, and exploring the ways in which our thoughts and emotions influence our behavior. It may also involve working on developing more positive self-talk and focusing on the good in others and in ourselves.

Finally, it is important to practice forgiveness in small ways

every day, such as by letting go of minor irritations and embracing a more compassionate and understanding attitude.
This can help to build resilience and to foster a growth
mindset, making it easier to forgive others and ourselves in
more challenging situations.

In conclusion, forgiveness is a key aspect of personal growth
and development, and it is closely tied to our mindset. A
growth mindset, characterized by a belief in personal
growth, resilience, and the ability to change, can help us to
cultivate a spirit of forgiveness and compassion, leading to
greater peace, well-being, and happiness. By practicing
mindfulness, self-reflection, and small acts of forgiveness,
we can develop the skills and attitudes needed to embrace a
more positive and forgiving outlook.

35: The Mindset of a Champion: Unleashing Your Potential

A champion mindset is a positive, growth-oriented outlook that drives individuals to achieve their goals and reach their full potential. This mindset is characterized by a strong sense of self-belief, resilience, and a relentless pursuit of excellence. Champions view obstacles as opportunities for growth and understand that success is a journey, not a destination.

The first step in developing a champion mindset is to cultivate a strong sense of self-belief. This means that you must believe in yourself, your abilities, and your potential to succeed. This self-belief must be unshakable, even in the face of adversity. A champion mindset requires you to be confident in your abilities and trust in your own judgment.

In addition to self-belief, champions possess resilience and determination. They understand that success requires hard work and persistence. They do not give up when faced with challenges, but instead use these experiences to fuel their growth and improvement. Champions are also driven by a relentless pursuit of excellence, constantly pushing themselves to be the best they can be.

Another important aspect of a champion mindset is a focus on personal growth. Champions are always seeking ways to improve, both in their personal and professional lives. They are lifelong learners, constantly seeking new knowledge and skills to help them reach their goals. They understand that success is a journey, not a destination, and that growth is an ongoing process.

To develop a champion mindset, it is important to surround yourself with positive and supportive people. This can include family, friends, mentors, and peers. These people can help you stay focused on your goals and provide encouragement and motivation when you need it. It is also important to cultivate a growth-oriented environment, filled with opportunities for learning and personal development.

Finally, champions practice mindfulness and self-reflection. They understand that their thoughts and attitudes have a powerful impact on their life and success. By regularly practicing mindfulness and self-reflection, they are able to stay centered and focused, even in the face of challenges.

In conclusion, the mindset of a champion is a powerful tool for success and personal growth. By cultivating a strong sense of self-belief, resilience, and a relentless pursuit of excellence, you can unleash your potential and achieve your goals. By surrounding yourself with positive people, focusing on personal growth, and practicing mindfulness, you can develop a champion mindset and live a life filled with success and happiness.

36: Conclusion: Living a Life of Mindset Mastery

In this chapter, we will discuss the importance of mastering your mindset and how it can impact every aspect of your life. A growth mindset, characterized by a belief in the ability to develop and improve through effort, has been shown to lead to greater success, happiness, and fulfillment. Conversely, a fixed mindset, characterized by a belief in inherent abilities, can limit personal growth and potential.

In order to live a life of mindset mastery, it is important to understand and embrace the power of your thoughts and beliefs. This means recognizing the impact your mindset has on your perception of success and failure, embracing challenges as opportunities for growth, and being mindful of negative thoughts and beliefs. By transforming your mindset, you can unlock your full potential and achieve your goals and aspirations.

One of the key strategies for developing a growth mindset is to challenge yourself regularly. This could mean taking on new challenges, trying new things, or pushing yourself to do something that is outside of your comfort zone. By constantly seeking new challenges, you can continue to grow and develop as a person.

Another important strategy for developing a growth mindset is to embrace failure as a path to growth and success. Rather than viewing failure as a setback, it is important to understand that it is a natural part of the learning and growth process. By embracing failure and viewing it as a valuable opportunity for growth, you can become more resilient and achieve greater success in life.

Gratitude is also a powerful tool for shaping your mindset. By focusing on the things you are grateful for, you can cultivate a positive and optimistic outlook on life. This can help you to overcome negative thoughts and beliefs, and live a life of happiness and fulfillment.

Mindfulness is another key practice for mindset transformation. By being present in the moment and focusing on your thoughts, emotions, and experiences, you can gain a deeper understanding of your thoughts and beliefs, and cultivate a more positive and growth-oriented mindset.

Finally, the role of mindset in building strong relationships cannot be overstated. By approaching relationships with a growth mindset, you can foster deeper connections and build stronger, more meaningful relationships.

In conclusion, mastering your mindset is a critical component of living a fulfilling and successful life. By embracing a growth mindset and utilizing strategies such as challenging yourself, embracing failure, practicing gratitude, mindfulness, and building strong relationships, you can unlock your full potential and live a life of mindset mastery.

Thank You

As we reach the end of this book, I want to say thanks for reading this book.

I want to get this information out to as many people as possible. If you found this book helpful, I would greatly appreciate you leaving me a review. This helps others find the book as well.

Disclaimer

This document is geared towards providing exact and reliable information in regards to the topic and issue covered. The publication is sold on the idea that the publisher is not required to render an accounting, officially permitted, or otherwise, qualified services. If advice is necessary, legal, financial, medical or professional, a practiced individual in the profession should be ordered.

This information is not presented by a financial or medical practitioner and is for entertainment, educational and informational purposes only. The content is not intended as a substitute for professional medical advice, diagnosis, or treatment. Always seek the advice of your physician or other qualified health care provider with any questions you may have regarding a medical condition. Never disregard professional medical advice or delay in seeking it because of something you have read.

The information provided herein is stated to be truthful and consistent, in that any liability, in terms of inattention or otherwise, by any usage or abuse of any policies, processes, or directions contained within is the solitary and utter responsibility of the recipient reader. Under no circumstances

DISCLAIMER

will any legal responsibility or blame be held against the publisher for any reparation, damages, or monetary loss due to the information herein, either directly or indirectly.

www.ingramcontent.com/pod-product-compliance
Lightning Source LLC
Chambersburg PA
CBHW060332130626
46553CB00003B/989